AMERICAN
DREAM
WITH EXIT
WOUND

AMERICAN DREAM WITH EXIT WOUND

Dawn McGuire

IF
SF
publishing

First Edition

ISBN 978-0-9859773-7-5

Published by IF SF Publishing
San Francisco, California
www.ifsfpublishing.com

Cover and Book Design by
David Barich, San Francisco, California

Acknowledgments

With appreciation to the following journals, print and/or web, and anthologies in which some of these poems have appeared, sometimes in previous versions: *Consequences Magazine, Cyclamens and Swords, Journal of the American Medical Association (JAMA), Jung Journal, Neurology: Journal of the American Academy of Neurology, Narrative Magazine, The New Yorker (podcast), Nimrod International, Talking Writing, The American Dream Anthology, The Montreal Poetry Prize Anthology*

Special thanks to Elinor Armer, Anita Barrows, Joan Baranow, Judy Halebsky, Jeffrey Levine, Claudia Monpere, David Shaddock and Barbara Tomash, for your deep reading and encouragement; and to Brooks Roddan and David Barich for your faith in this book.

DEDICATION

To my Patients: Veterans of Foreign Wars and the Wars at Home

CONTENTS

Invocation to the Muse 11

HAZARDOUS MATERIALS.. 12

Hazmat..15
65th and Telegraph 16
Isis in Eddyville 17
Watertown Nights 18
Special Ops...19
Ecce Homo...20
Ubershadow 22
Situation Room 23
American Dream with Exit Wound 24
After Finding a Firefighter's Ax at the Thrift Store 26

LIMBICS...28

Found...31
Jealousy 32
Tin Star.. 34
Love in the Skilled Nursing Unit 35
Juvenalia 36
Another Fragment 31 38
An-Elegy 39
Essentials 40
Antipode..41
Looking Closely...42
Ode to Entropy 44
My Friend is Convinced it's the Turmeric 46
You've Got Mail... 48
The Same Thing Happened in Iconium.................................49
Orbe...50
Ode to Gears 52
Absolutely...54

GHOSTS..56

Everything About the Subject 59
Gorilla Dreams 60
Text for Two Deserts 61
Crossing Conditions..62
Kin..64
Consistently Wrong 65
Brain at Dusk..66
Diastema..68
On Polishing 69
Brother H and Sister Bitch..70
Ghost...72
I Am Almost the Street 74
If You Can't See My Mirrors 75
On the Immortality of the Soul.................................76
Listen to the Birds 78

INVOCATION TO THE MUSE

You're a bony, rangy old thing
asking for love

You go to your desk
and worry a line, worry a line

Flat-footed, crick in your neck
What a rickety mess

Never think for a second
I don't want you

HAZARDOUS MATERIALS

"The tremendous war goes on. Every family has directly or indirectly some representative among this vast army of the wounded and sick."

—**Walt Whitman,** *New York Times,* December 11, 1864

HAZMAT

Choose one of the six plots
four ironies, eleven conflicts
and a point of view. The guy
in the theater sits under a ceiling
painted with day-glow constellations.
Isadora Duncan is wrapping her scarf
around Orion's belt.
He's waiting for mayhem or the feature
film, scrolling through email, listening
with one ear to previews.
His good ear, the other
a rag of eardrum, incus in bits,
stapes shot to shit.

Operation
Enduring Freedom
He's lucky, his cousin said,
to have made it back without a prosthesis.
It's a romantic comedy.
They wouldn't let his service dog in
(he forgot the special vest) but no big.
Vulcan can sleep in the truck.
As long as there's no loud noise.
At this point laughing's ok.
Ten years of chick flicks
and in real life he still
can't trust himself
with a girl.

65TH AND TELEGRAPH

My friend Mary Claire
not the one with gout
the one with cancer

raised chickens in Oakland.
She built a beautiful—what do they call it—
a coop (a fine Cape Cod, $39 plans)

from recovered wood. She had some
good cedar, ash, poplar
from her brother's little league bat.

The roosts were perfectly leveled
when they arrived: Alpha Alice,
Petite Coquette, Becky and Beckett.

At dusk they'd bicker and fuss
until she opened the coop,
then up the ramp they'd go.

Once on the roost, they were set
for the night, hard-wired
to clutch the bar until dawn.

The guy who stole them
must have had a time that night
ungripping their feet.

He gave up on Alice.
She probably broke some skin.
By the time M. C. made it

into the yard, he was already
down Telly.
"Even from the back,"

she was crying,
"you could tell how
fucking hungry he was."

ISIS IN EDDYVILLE

My sister could never keep the truth
close to her chest like the rest of us.
Her face would flush, her lips swell

until she'd have to call us in.
We'd huddle in a clot in the bedroom
braiding each other's hair, waiting

for the stink bomb to drop.
We'd start to wheeze and tear.
You'd think we'd run

but we'd stay, choking,
holding our noses in that last
smelly temple of our girlhood.

She was our Isis.
The one who finally told us
our brother was not in college

but in Rehab.
And, *no,* daddy didn't run
the House of the Lord in Kenya

but Sunday School at the Kentucky
State Pen. And it wasn't really Jesus
who sent food stamps.

After that, one of us
would always go with her
to stand in line.

WATERTOWN NIGHTS

Tonight I wake up clammy and anginal after rushing from
door to door. Behind one is smoke and scald; the other opens
to pastoral green relief that it's not me or mine in terrorist
bits in Boston or Belgium;

but as unbearable, this kind of bad-faith adipose happiness that
makes me pass the bathroom mirror and not want to look.

I go back to sleep and wake up in Watertown. The police say,
Stay inside! Don't open your door!

The teenager in the white cap, is he the rough beast, the
hour narrowing? Or just another Ares-devoured son? *Shh.*
Shelter in place

the Captain says and I want to believe him.
His gleaming gold star, his megaphone, his promise
of guidance as the night goes on.

SPECIAL OPS

They can control the drones
from almost anywhere now.
In a sound-proof, bomb-grade
studio by the Potomac
they watch birds dive the dock
after fishermen clean their haul

while three screens triangulate
on a donkey in Ma'rib.
Its huge stupid head
tolls over a patch of grass,
an image not without tenderness.
Except it's been a few weeks

without the sign of a kill
to show the Force
is with us.
Snatch that last
mouthful, pal.
Sorry, sorry

ECCE HOMO

He keeps trying to bring

the Classics back to life

for his son. *You're like Oedipus,*

he says. *You can't help*

what you're doing. But a man's

still accountable.

His son listens as long as he can.

They wait on the bench

at the detox clinic.

What use are the blues?

Notes bent on a guitar

made from the wood-hard

veins in a son's arms.

Now he shoots up

in his feet.

He nods off as his father

starts the intell on Antigone:

It's like no soldier

left behind, you know?

he whispers.

Khe Sanh '68.

His son, Bagram 2012,

pawned his father's Purple Heart

for some high-end Afghani smack.

There's a tragedy

a minute, Nietzsche says.

He's next on the list

after the Greeks.

You know what a man would give.

Every donate-able organ.

His life's last glance.

To know what to fix.

To know how. Not even why.

UBERSHADOW

You cough into your arm the way the sign says
but your shadow spews microbials into the crowd
is how you find out.

You fix your hair; your shadow's hair
sticks out. You know you sewed the hem
your shadow's ripping.

Your shadow's slipping off to assignations
while you try to sleep.
Who can sleep? A shady you—

shape is making the rounds,
cutting deals, using your body,
using your name.

What to do
about what's being done
in your name.

SITUATION ROOM

This ransom idea has caught on.
The boot on your tire.
The loan on your home.

The war in your name.
Oh, and we have your daughter.
Her dinner is parsley and water;

her breakfast: fitbit.
All day long in the mirror:
Scale and Gaze.

Your son's in Khost Province
lugging ROTC debt and an 80-pound pack
that wrecks his knee.

Oxy works wonders in the field.
Back home, heroin's cheaper.
Easier to get.

Rehab, relapse, rehab.
Every bedroom, ransom.
Every day the war.

AMERICAN DREAM WITH EXIT WOUND

She looks at belts differently now
Not at the grain, the tool work

Not thinking what size for which waist
She looks at where the holes are

One punched out with a nail file
a peeler, dug out with a stick

blunt but strong enough
to grind out a hole in leather

A hole too close to the buckle

She looks at his belts for a hole
too close to the buckle

Belt, tourniquet, cinch—
The cubital vein pops up

blue as a bruise
a swollen lip

The sting is brief
endurable

And all that is unendurable
melts into air

Hectoring voices
stilled

Enemies pierced
through

Achilles at last asleep in his tent
His pillow wet

The warm, blue Aegean
slipping over it

AFTER FINDING A FIREFIGHTER'S AX
AT THE THRIFT STORE

It is not enough to know the word
for this or that kind of fire.
Lightning fire, controlled burn,
slash and brush, arson,
the crown fire at the tops of trees,
branches entwined, raging as the one
red, many- headed God of State
ignites the next war.

                    *

Now that the volunteer army's
such a suicidal mess, the Generals
recommend a draft.
If the sons and daughters
of the middle class aim the droids
and bomb the dots, they'll come home
to some options. They can work in the Firm,
join the service industry

get some help with the ghost smoke
in the attic, white phosphorous everywhere,
eternal vigilance. Flashback tanks
flatten Fallujah again and again;
sonic blasts and the deaf
roadside ritual
of the matching
of the parts—

*

After—
a kind of silence.

You have to put your back into it
and use the right tools

as when you make a fire line
with a Pulaski ax

scraping down
to the inflammable, mineral soil

to the silence
of Priam and Achilles

when finally they bent towards one another,
grieving their blood—

even Homer had no lines for it.

LIMBICS

limbic system—From Latin limbus, "edge." A group of interconnected structures in the brain common to all mammals; associated with primary emotional pigments: love and lust, rage and shame, grief and epiphany.

FOUND[1]

Every time I try to write about the body

the writing ends up

being about language.

This is not because I think

the body is

reducible

to language;

it is not. Language

emerges

from the body,

constituting an emission of sorts.

The body

is that upon which

language

falters,

and the body carries

its own signs.

---

1. Cento from Judith Butler's Undoing Gender (2004).

JEALOUSY

I'm drinking *vino tinto* in front of
a three-story dog made of flowers.
The old distractions fail me.
They even make things worse.

I try a church and end up
cheeking the communion wafer
like Thorazine as the white gowns
glide past. Holy water splashes
in and out of suppressed coves.

I pick up a book I once loved,
reread how Anytus risked his life
to bring the Thirty Tyrants down,
democracy back to Athens, then
rushed to sentence Socrates
to death.

             What chance
do any of us have against
desire? His handsome Alcibiades
loved Socrates more.

Even with enough white matter
to circle twice the Earth,
we kill for love.
The neocortex can loom large,
harsh as an exhausted mother
saying use your words use your words

but your amygdala's in flames.
Anytus is ravenous, and Socrates,
a bent old man the dogs jump on,
is looking like Adonis.

We're wired like this.
My grandfather, a gentle Christian man,
at 92 still remembered how rich bankers
used to come around the farm,
circle and sniff his Helen.

Sixty years, and he still
kept a pipe wrench in his boot.

TIN STAR

I see them in myself, the two alpha females
fighting with their carts, plunging bad
grammar into soft tissue; the kid—
which one did he belong to? is starting
to cry, not so anyone can hear.
I barely notice him myself, his little
tin star, his head just big enough
to cover with a hand.

They shout until they're wheezing
and I'm wheezing, and I'm thinking
how you're never all one thing;
how I want one of them to win
then the other; how I want this
even as the little guy is putting his
Cheez Whiz back, hunkering
in the aisle until they're done.

LOVE IN THE SKILLED
NURSING UNIT

After Sappho's Fragment 31

Whacked with a bat
in Dolores Park for his wallet,
Ari can't make new memories.
All day he lives in Then,

except when his wife of three
decades stands in the doorway.
In her dun-colored muumuu,
sandals from Thrift-Co
that leave enough room
for her hammertoes,
she's Aphrodite.

He whoops and sighs,
tries to unlock his Geri-chair,
his face flushed, then pale
as maiden grass.

Suddenly he's mute—
his tongue,
broken by beauty.

That's when I'd give
my temporal lobe,
my hippocampus whole,
for his cheap blue gown;

to gaze upon that love again
by which one is first made,
inflamed, destroyed—

then raised
to aerial ash
again and again.

JUVENALIA²

The kids overhear us talking in the kitchen
about the Bitter End on Bleeker, and Folk City,
where homeless teenage Dylan slept
on the floor in back. The manager
was always kind like that.

Even now in the kitchen he's helping
our girl band haul axes and amps into a taxi
we can't afford, but it's 3 a.m.
They'd be jacked on the subway.
My bass isn't even paid for.

Somewhere between Thompson and LaGuardia
Jen wants a baby; Daisanne gets a writing gig
at the *Voice;* and Phiale—gray-eyed Phiale,
who could give the hardest heart
an aching hard on, goes home

to her man in Detroit.
I go back to study axons.
By now the kids' jaws have gone slack
as the strings on the bass
in the basement.

The smooth tune of their universe
just dropped from treble clef.
They're churning, I can see it,
wondering what else
they never knew—

*Come in, don't hover
in the doorway.*

I'll always be yours.
I won't leave my estate to Phiale.

> *(so careless her song;*
> *the fortune we spent*
> *in her narrow archway)*

2. Phiale, in Juvenal's *Satires,* seduces rich old men

ANOTHER FRAGMENT 31

I open my refrigerator and find
The Stop Violence Coalition News
next to the figs and lemon curd.
I spread fear for my world on
five-grain bread from Whole Earth Foods.

Isn't hope a sweet, fat fig?
The tiny fig wasp crawls to the center
through a narrow ostiole.
Her antennae snap, her wings
shear off in the journey. Dying

in darkness, she lays her necessary
eggs, else the worlds of Wasp and Fig
expire. *Is there no beauty
without misfortune?* asks Baudelaire.
Surely—yet,

her body, in each sweet, hypnotic
bite.

AN-ELEGY

In the middle of life's journey
I called my first love in Stockholm.
Who are you? she asked.

As there is no Swedish equivalent
for *oo,* it came out: *Wyü are yü?*

That's why I called, I said.
Untranslatable plosive,
she replied. *I can't believe it's yü!*

Such a relief, I said.
I thought I was dead.

Of course, Sophocles horned in:
You can't go back in an elegy!
ε, λεγε ε, λεγε: Woe, cry woe, cry!

Yet, here we are climbing her stairs
in the dark again. This far North,
nights start early, last long.

The polished bannister leading up
is as slick to the touch as a marble
rolled in oil.

ESSENTIALS

We were in Buzini, or it could have been Mlini,

one of those hamlets in the disputed territories,

with the hundred-proof potato schnapps

combusting in our throats, mid-spat

(the bitter one begun in Montenegro)

when I stripped and jumped into the Dragonja.

It was December and you leapt in after.

The two of us then, blue, chattering,

bradycardic, sharps of the ancient

riverbed tearing our feet.

We clung naked as elements

to each other's skin. All

the superfluous rest of us

washed down to the Bay of Piran.

ANTIPODE

When I finally realize any sign

eventually turns to its opposite

and asks forgiveness

sleep comes easily

I make a bed by the delta

pull Orion down for heat

and dreamless, sleep

even as peril sets up camp

under the freeway

Already tomorrow's news

is pulling on its rough ski mask

What defense, your body

that completes me under sheets of stars

Hands that unwrap me like a gift

No defense. Joy consubstantial

with the fear that asks forgiveness

even as it rips and tears, even as it shears

Orion from Aurora's side

LOOKING CLOSELY

I loved talking to the big guy after
the reading

He had that taut, central meniscus of fat
you see in middle age

covered by a lime-colored IZOD
polo shirt in its third life

paisley shorts from 1969
I don't remember his name

but could draw the arthroscopy scar
on his left knee, the mole on his neck

which looked entirely benign
(or I would have said something)

*You know a good dermatologist
in Iowa City?*

*

He talked about Gertrude Stein, the Harlem Renaissance, nuns
on the bus. We trekked the Icelandic rim, forgot the reception,
all four of our hemispheres amped on dopamine ice cream

*

Still—
I would still have intruded—

with regret—
but the mole looked benign

*

But sometimes you can't tell
Maybe I'll email him anyway

     *

I can never stay long in heaven

I was trained to be this way

I already was this way

A twist of mental nature, always asking

what if I'm completely

catastrophically

wrong

An epistemological birthmark that scares children

We're all children

     *

It's back to the cell block: *Anxiety*

What if I said nothing
and was wrong

No clear path
How could there be a path

Everything comes in twos
and halves of twos

and the wheel can't help but wheel

ODE TO ENTROPY

Cords—
Take any two
they tangle

Alignment and order
exist past tense
says the Law

Even the sushi master's rice
lined up, exact as dipole moments
each grain facing North

hides flukes that want a piece of you
Wabi sabi
Rust and ruin world

By now you know
the pretty cabana boy
who wants to friend you

will bitter your sweet drink
and tag your car
His aerosol script as indecipherable

as memory
the cipher you reel in
from a different river every time

This moment's monofilament line
pulls up the bomber jacket
you kept on for her, endless night

then sealed in an airless
waterproof keep
at absolute zero

wanting to fix the sweat-sex
leather like a fact of Nature
A continuous whole

By now you know
how memory falls
from the hanger of your body

odorless

Sugar side chains cleaved
Cell membranes split into seams

Broken the covalent

The leather—still high quality

but without family

much too cold to touch

MY FRIEND IS CONVINCED IT'S THE TURMERIC

keeping his glioblastoma in check,
not the Avastin, not the *-ex's* and *-ides,*
not the expertly directed killer rays

but a hermaphroditic rhizome
the color of monks' robes,
bees' feet in pollen.

On his scans, voxels of drama:
the Hun's army about to cross the Rhine,
plunge into Paris. Already flaming arrows

glance off the baby grand.
Drugged, he thinks they are lovely
My red-tailed comets, he says

and goes for more hummingbird food.
Stacks of Fauré and Debussy singe.
He puts out the wisps with his thumb.

This was how it was found:
One day he smelled smoke
in his brain.

His left hand is still too weak
for the Romantics, but somewhere
between the Plains of Catalaunia

and the right ventricle of his brain
Attila has turned back.
In every room, turmeric.

Rhizomes on seed trays, tooth-bud up;
a hemic smell, like battle.
Everywhere, orange stains:

on scores he's never far from,
on keys that deliver his tender blows
to the strings' steel core.

YOU'VE GOT MAIL

Eat This, Never Die
was in my inbox with a photo-
shopped scene of the Last
Supper with kale and quinoa
on Peter's plate.

I was listening
to Mahalia Jackson
and knew I should take it all
to Jesus. Today it's punctual
acres of weeds to pull

when I can't even get out of bed.
In Death Valley it's torrid, but here
that's no excuse: it's mild with
oaks appliquéd to sky, a sun-blocking
canopy. Tuesday a wood rat

slipped into the bird feeder
as I watched. His tiny teeth
glee'd around mounds of warbler seed.
O, happy day! Stuffed,
he jumped back down

as a short-eared owl swooshed
from oak camouflage
and carried him off like a purse.
Best day, last day.
That's how I hope it goes.

No substitute for death, is there?
The feeder still swinging;
the way things are.
Time to get up.
Mow and sow.

THE SAME THING HAPPENED
IN ICONIUM,

the carriage passing by in the fog
with my whole
vocabulary

Every word: doubt, denial,
persuasion,
the lyric of last resort

torn apart at the joint

hauled away
The fleshy family units of the town cheer
The draft horse strains

At the dock, the flagman raises the flag
Its anemic pigments wave
over the garbage barge

It gets hard to breathe alone   Alone
is the pale yellow dog
barking at cars

The neighbors say they worry
but no one sets out a bowl
What is worry but a word?   Yet my tongue
slips over the lip of it

and I sip

ORBE

This morning the van pulled up
with four of my limbic themes

but I stayed in the hot tub.
They'll keep.

Mother, Money, God and Sex
have the shelf-life of titanium.

With my lover's son in rehab,
safe for now, we have more

than a moment by moment
futurity.

Once I believed
in a kind of tragic alienation

not in this cold, polar
evacuation of meaning.

Good is very sorry about it
and blows on her piccolo.

If skimmed milk could whistle
it would sound like that.

If our boy ends up in the Kingdom
of China White, at least

he won't be lonely.
Brian, who first shot him up,

Ben and Kayla Marie
are preparing a place for him.

We talk about moving to Orbe
in the Swiss Canton of Vaud

where heroin's legal.
Just soak

the doctor says.
You can't save anyone.

ODE TO GEARS

I rarely see you anymore. Even bikes
are going gearless, along with the gear-
grease wiped on jeans like forever stamps.
I miss the grease—*no*—
I miss the confidence that once again
the damn van will run.

Some bubblegum, a rubber band.
Rub the dirty spark plugs on your pants,
crawl under the block, attitude-back
the stripped bolt, yank it out like a tooth.
Rust flakes drift down like dried blood.
Gears and grease—

in the mnemic suitcase we carry,
still 19 and hungry, every part
of the one artichoke between us
consumed, still hungry, stirring
the morning's ashes,
we're walking on air like ashes.

The van did break
and the tent collapsed.
And weren't we smooth
slipping from first to third
even without a clutch?
A continuum, we imagined;

in the inwardness,
in the eye of things.

We were quiet so as to know it.
We listened to nothing there
and prepared.

ABSOLUTELY

There will be troubles.
Night will stay night.
At first you'll get angry
and pick a fight.

Your amygdala won't listen.
Your blood will acidify.
Gravity will call and your
cell phone will fall in the toilet.

              You'll take your troubles
to a shrink who'll recommend
a cruise and you'll sail to Bimini
and get giardia which the ship's doctor
will diagnose from across the room
when you burp up clouds of sulfur.

Home, your bedroom ceiling will leak,
roof rats will chew your sleep.
You'll try to leverage insomnia
and write about the troubles.
A starling will smack the window
and you'll startle out of your chair
and drop your laptop and won't even care.

There will be troubles
and you won't care and that's
the trouble your shrink will say
as you write your last anhedonic
check. You won't bother to curse
the memo line. You're still belching hell
and swallowing flagyl.

It's 2 a.m. and you're watching Frankenstein
reruns again. Not because Boris Karloff
is like the father you never had
but like your father.

He has troubles
everyone says. His rough hands
crush the Black-Eyed Susans
he rips out of the ground for you,
which tonight remind you, with absolute
certainty, you have been loved, are
absolutely safe.

GHOSTS

EVERYTHING ABOUT THE SUBJECT

but not the subject comes home here.

The word *body* enters the body
converts its substance

swallows its air. Pitch and silence
define the body now.

Slick reticular switchbacks
convey what you say.

Diverticular crypts
hide what you hide.

When my son suckled
he hummed. When hungry he cried.

Where is my body's endless milk?
Its wordless fleece?

Tonight, hand over mouthpiece,
stifled, his cry.

GORILLA DREAMS

They walk on their knuckles
towards your binoculars.
You can pay the big bucks
and live in a tent for a week
where a ranger will stand guard.
He'll risk a head shot from a 12 -year-old
soldier from Goma. Or the M23
will take you up for half price USD.

Last things in their neighborhoods
don't ask for a dime.
Go back to sleep.

In your red nightshirt,
nothing is foolish.

You're almost close enough
to touch them all.

TEXT FOR TWO DESSERTS

The last time I had anything to say
I didn't.

Everyone comments on how we look
so much alike. It's true—in part.

His hands, more elegant,
slower to storm. Mine rash and tear

at low-hanging clouds that scare me
like theater smoke. Yet, finally

I can tolerate the mystery of hands.
The mirror of our faces

let go. Stand down
before this uncanny

other: no-one's blue-eyed boy.
He hands me a glass of Prosecco

from his first legal stash,
adds a secret spice—maybe ginger?

which someone I may never meet
has taught him tastes like joy.

CROSSING CONDITIONS

I saw a half-ton bull moose nibbling a tree by the neon
Moose Crossing sign. At the lake, a beaver-cleaved birch.

By the highway towards Casper, fang marks
of oil rigs, exhausted scrabble surround. Last night

I dreamed of my old lover. He was still angry,
he gave me back my clothes.

I dream of him rarely now—was it the huge moose
with sensitive lips, millions of axons selecting the exact

green bud of his need? Or the blind perseverant penetration
of the rig?

I think the birch.
Almost chewed in two, bent near to breaking,

only an inch of pith between the halves.
One last gnaw, a push, then glide to the dam.

I imagine my lover with his Tom's Toothpaste teeth
laughing until he's crying; imagine

his sweet love delirium unharmed.
I dream of being undamned.

I wake up and settle for usefulness.
The steady *V* of the beaver's wake

as it crosses the current
towards the work to be done.

KIN

A blanket of holes, the smell of piss and sour milk, infection
is our love. After the dressings, kin-blisters continue to weep
though. At work, mid-meeting, the granny-assassin appears
with the family tax cheat, the horse thief, the slain child bride.
You doubt you can be trusted when push comes to shove and
don't want to study this.

Already you know that if you insert a blade into the common
seam, hear the snak-snak of parting planes, if you separate the
interstitium without drawing blood, still you go back to the
porch at night.

The whole clan's here. H.H. brings moonshine from Pactolus.
Rildy sets out fudge and cigarettes. The circle is lit by fireflies
in mason jars. Everyone knows where to sit, including the
dead. The ratio of circumference to diameter is physical,
mystical, unresolvable. We are sealed in. We laugh as one;
our lighters flick in unison.

CONSISTENTLY WRONG

At 7 I knew
You weren't really gone

You were coming back
(in 7 years)

After 7 years
Famine

The next 7
The next

Then when you came
into my room as if you'd never left

With your root beer float and your eternity
and asked if you could have our father, too

I said Yes
and also Here

Take this choker
I wore for you

It's too small
It never grew

BRAIN AT DUSK

Dusk falls like a minor third
the interval of regret
The backyard hangs with tongues
of speechless sheets

not dry, not wet
Not night, not day

A mute third thing is 6 p.m.
A blister of emptiness

My father is always twelve
this time of day
Earlier he sneaked away
from the brickyard to go to school

He'll come home to a whipping
as usual. As usual I can't
do anything from here

Night arrives with bruises
and the complicated stars

*

My father becomes
an educated man
who shouts in his sleep

He never raises a hand to me
Not anger
Not tenderness

He teaches me the names of stars
About Orion, whom Aurora loved,
who cleared the beasts off Chios

Dear Neocortex:
Gripped, tight as a fist
around your diamond sky
why talk empty-handed?

DIASTEMA

I thought there must be a secret.

I felt it not there, kept feeling for it, everything toothy and

mouthy, wherever my tongue

went there was

the gap. I wanted

to put my hand over my mouth.

Where it wouldn't come together I was ashamed.

The little pied dog wants my attention, attention, attention.

Incurable is his hope. When he falls asleep under my hand

Everything meets.

ON POLISHING

Worst thing ever I did
was try to make things better.
Eliot was right. Wait.

This stainless silk,
this life, how easy
to wreck the finish.

BROTHER H AND SISTER BITCH

Downtown calls it Brown Sugar

Junk, Thunder

The stuff in the blackened spoon

He calls it

My Dearest Friend

Brother

(When he's in detox, it's Hell Dust)

*

His shrink calls it

a misguided attempt at transcendence

We thank him for that

*

Earth, air, water, exhaustion

We mostly stick to one room

like Army wives

dreading the knock, the call

*

These narrative constructs are garments

the moths chew on

*

He texts from detox

I'm good. Really. Please

be at peace

He adds a golden sun emoticon

*

Naked, we know better.

A longhand letter is under his bed:

I'll be with you again soon

Insidious Bitch.

Be kind.

Finish me off this time.

GHOST

Did you ever notice in Hamlet that
the wrong sentry asks
Who's there?

Not the one on duty
but the one
just coming on?

As if startled from sleep
The way I come into my father's room
after a storm wind rattles the oak

It scratched at the roof just now
I come in to his room asking
Who's there?

Afraid he will ask me
who I am

      *

Pound says the light sings eternal
in the finished husk

Does it really matter
if he's wrong?

      *

Catastrophe starts another
form of life

They look the same in a tux
They wear the same size

*

a figure; slippage—
words that bring you back so exactly
by so failing to

I Am Almost the Street

All the prints of the feet
would be indelible

if I were the street

But I am only almost
the street

I don't complain
when machines come at night

with hoses and self-
squirting soap

to scrub the day's footfalls
from my brain

By dawn I don't remember
any of them

Which ones ran,
running late

which dragged their feet
dreading arriving—

The whole day
drains to the Bay

Another no one
recalls surviving

IF YOU CAN'T SEE MY MIRRORS, I CAN'T SEE YOU

Say this life rides on the back of a piebald mare.

Not mythic, not descended from Stonewall Jackson's mount.
Nobody's archetype.

Of course, there are props:
a little dog with winged paws,
the plastic hibiscus.

In the background
a thematic hunger
no takeout can touch.

Time.
Time.
Feast and famine.

Say this ride is a mare.
You barely know a hands-width
of her back.

"On The Immortality Of The Soul"

after Plato's *Phaedo*

The ship is back from Delos.
The punishment may proceed.
Plato is sick (so he says)
but Phaedo, Cebes and I—
yes and weepy Apollodorus—
meet in the cell.

The guard unlocks the chains.
    Pleasure and pain
Socrates says, rubbing his legs
how twinned they are.

The whole day he argues
his body away.

    It's ivy around an oak
he says, *choking the soul.*

    In the Hymns
the slain go to the birds.
Let buzzards feast. No crying!

Apollodorus swallows a sob.

It will not even be your Socrates
whose legs go numb when the hemlock
makes its rounds!

A gadfly released
from its bottle is Socrates.

We ask ignorant questions
to stretch out the day.
Dusk comes anyway.
The guard starts mashing
the fleshy roots and seeds.

Socrates pays him no mind:

If all evidence eludes us,
if reason is just an old draft horse
Hades has brought to its knees,
we'll go with our best bet, Simmias.

Even Pythagoras was sure he heard
his best friend barking in that mangy old dog.

LISTEN TO THE BIRDS

This is all I have to say,
my heartbroken friend.
Not that you speak the language.
There is no language that makes sense
of living then dying.
My son says my hand becomes
a bear's paw batting the air when
I'm emphatic. It's the hand
of my father, hand of the seven
passions, limbic annotator
of this life's force as it yields,
imprecisely, to words.

At holiday table, the old engineer
says, "If I didn't make things
that make noise, I'd disappear."
The composer says, "I *am* my noise."
At dawn, birds awaken me
with their tonic whistles and tics.
We are not separate.
My father as he batted away
his last air said, "Don't be afraid."

A NOTE ON THE TYPE

The text face is Granjon, designed by George William Jones.
The headings are set in Charlemagne designed by
Carol Twombly at Adobe Systems Inc. in 1989.

Book and Cover Design by
David Barich, San Francisco, California